NOTHING WASTED

A True Story of Immigration and Resilience in Pursuit of the American Dream

DR. KAMA THOMAS

First published by Kama Thomas Consulting LLC
978-0-578-85793-0

Library of Congress Control Number: 2021908946

Printed in the United States of America

Kama Thomas Consulting LLC
P.O. Box 242253
Milwaukee, WI,53224
https://kamathomas.com

Memoir, Inspiration, Faith & Spirituality, Education

DISCLAIMER

This book is a memoir based on my recollection of events. I have endeavored to tell my story in an honest way that leaves everyone with their dignity. There are no villains in this story.

For every immigrant, every student, every dreamer
everywhere whose stories seldom get told.
You are seen. You are heard.

For my mother, my grandfather, and for St. Lucia.

CONTENTS

CHAPTER 1

A FULL HOUSE

"**K**AMA!" HE SAID MY name gently yet firmly, and I knew it was my grandfather calling for me. I answered loudly, "Yes, Papa," and ran up the concrete steps of our house to find him sitting at the table, finishing his dinner. I knew that whatever was left on his plate was for me. He did this with every meal, especially if it was something I loved eating. I would abandon whatever game I was playing outside, usually teaching my mother's plants whatever lesson I had learned in class that day.

My grandfather, my mother's father, was the first man to ever love me. He was a man of few words, but he was compassionate, kind, and generous. What I remember most about him is his incredible work ethic. It was unmatched. He would awaken at the crack of dawn, while the roosters and chickens were hardly awake, to go to his shop. Each day, he came home for lunch and then returned to his small rum shop to work, usually until six in the evening. When I walked in to visit him there, the smell of alcohol was the first thing to hit me. Men of various ages stood near the counter buying drinks, usually not their first for the day. When they got unruly, my grandfather firmly escorted them out. At some point in the day, someone would show up trying to sell something — blankets, sheets, fruits, random things. Often, my grandfather brought home treats for me, whatever was being sold that day.

His generosity knew no bounds, and I particularly loved when he went into the city, Castries, for a doctor's visit. He would return with juicy red plums, apples, or ackees. If anyone asked whether they could have some, he would reply, usually in Creole, "No, those all belong to Kama. Do not touch them!" He always took my side, spoke up in my defense, and championed my dreams. He loved me fiercely.

My older cousin Sherlan told me a story once. "Kama, do you know that Papa gave me a Malta from his shop for you one day, and he followed me all the way to the house to make sure that I hadn't drank any out of it?" I had not known this, but I wasn't surprised she remembered the moment so many years after his passing.

My grandfather often asked to look through my workbooks from school. He did this throughout my entire primary school career, until I was twelve years old. Once I was older, I realized he was looking for the number of questions I had gotten correct on my exams. With the biggest smile on his face, he encouraged me to keep improving, and when he noticed wrong answers, he gently reassured me of my capabilities. He was deeply invested in my education, and the smile radiating from his face when I brought home an excellent report card was worth all my hard work. A complete sense of joy overtook him. I now understand my commitment to excellence and achievement was birthed in the walls of my childhood home. If my achievements could bring him such joy, then I was determined to never let him down.

Although she passed away when I was quite young, probably about six years old, I also have very vivid memories of my maternal grandmother. She cared deeply for me, and, it seemed, for everyone else around her as well. I do wish I could have made more memories with her. In the memories I have, she allowed me to sit on her lap in the balcony of my childhood home and she fed me. My mother told me years later that my grandmother was also a generous woman who gave of her gifts, talents, and time to villagers. She was considered a medicine woman, and although she had no formal training, her knowledge of natural medicines and homeopathic remedies for any ailment was vast. She frequently visited sick villagers to provide them with care. "She would not leave until they were healed," my mother told me.

My grandmother was passionate about using natural herbs to heal the sick. She would stay with the ailing man, woman, or child until she found a cure for whatever their issue was. Sometimes, it took all day and night. She was famous for removing fish bones that were stuck in villagers' throats or foreign objects from the ears of children, and she was a woman of faith, so she prayed before each procedure she performed.

My grandmother was a woman of great strength who also owned her own business. In this way, she was ahead of her time, since few women owned businesses at that place and time. My grandmother sold an assortment of cakes and baked and fried foods in her shop. She fed hundreds of people in her lifetime. When the football team from my village returned from winning a tournament, one of their first stops would be her shop. She fed them all for free as a way to commend them for their achievement.

I grew up in Anse-la-Raye, a tiny fishing village on the island of St. Lucia. Anse-la-Raye was a unique place where most of the men were fishermen. They went out to sea very early in the mornings and returned in the afternoons with a variety of fish in heavy nets to sell near the beach. My village was about a thirty-minute drive from the capital of Castries, and it was a quiet place most days. On Sunday mornings, the sound of the bells of the towering Catholic church announcing nine o'clock Mass penetrated the air and could be heard on all sides of the village.

Most of the village was Catholic, and if you were really religious, you went back to Mass in the evenings at six o'clock for prayer. There was also early morning prayer at six during the week. Mass was a way of life, especially as we prepared for the sacraments of First Holy Communion or Confirmation. The only time I missed Mass on Sundays was if I was gravely ill. My mom made sure my siblings and I went every Sunday. My brother even had the experience of becoming an altar boy when he was old enough. I always made sure I stood in his line when I walked up to the altar to receive communion because I knew he wouldn't be able to keep a straight face as I stuck my tongue out and made faces at him.

The beach was a one-minute walk from the Catholic church, and the infant school, Anse-la-Raye Roman Catholic School, often felt like it was an extension of the church. There was also a primary school in my village, which students started attending at around nine years old. The primary school was closer to the rivers, and we had to walk about fifteen minutes from our house to get there.

Saturdays were usually laundry days, and women and children could be seen walking to the river with large blue tubs of clothes on their heads. This could be an all-day task depending on how much laundry needed to be done. It was a simple life; it was all we knew and we were content.

I lived in a calypso green house, which seemed to always be full, on Bridge Street. There were four bedrooms, a working bathroom, and running water. Even at a young age, I was aware of some of my privileges. My closest friends had to use a public bathroom and walked to the community standpipe to collect water several times a day.

My grandmother, grandfather, mother, older sister and brother, a family friend, several cousins, and I all lived under the same roof. Back then, it did not seem crowded. In fact, it seemed normal since it was a typical way of life for most villagers. A house was never too small to sleep more people even though it meant using old clothing to make our bed on the floor.

My father lived a few streets away and visited on the weekends, carrying the Saturday newspaper and sometimes a Heineken. What I remember most about my dad was the way he stressed the importance of an education to us. I was terrified of him. I was terrified of disappointing him, and so I chased achievement to no end. My friends must have suspected my siblings and I were afraid of our dad. Often, if we were playing in the front yard, they would notice him approaching before we did and would yell out, "Your father's coming! Your father's coming!" My sister, my brother, and I would run into the house, grab a book, and pretend to be reading or studying.

My father was also the most intelligent man I knew, and he had an intimidating vocabulary. He was easily disappointed if I could not provide answers to random trivia or math questions or questions about news stories. Although I was an avid reader who was seldom out of the presence of books, by the time I reached age eight, my mother thought it would be a good idea if my dad provided me with extra help with mathematics. I had to walk over to my paternal grandmother's house for the extra lessons after school, and as I went, anxiety welled up in me. I felt like a lamb walking to a slaughterhouse on Christmas Eve.

Thankfully, my half-sister, Heidi, my dad's daughter, came along with me sometimes. She was two years older than I was, and I could sense that she didn't look forward to an afternoon of math with our father either. "Kama, you know the answer!" he yelled when I hesitated to provide the answers to the questions quickly enough. His punishment was swift and sharp when my answers were wrong, and I walked home in defeat with red blotches on my legs as a reminder of each wrong answer. My father did not know any better, and for that, I have forgiven him. It was simply the way things were back then. Teachers and principals were also allowed to exercise corporal punishment, and we did not question it.

Education was a huge part of my life growing up. Both my father and grandfather expected me to excel academically without question. In fact, in summers, my father would buy me several books, and I would have to write a book report on each one. *A Tale of Two Cities, The Cloud with a Silver Lining,* and *Dr. Doolittle* are some of the titles I remember. Although I preferred to spend the summer playing outside, like all my friends, this is where my love for books and learning probably began.

By my ninth birthday, my father had moved to the United States to start a new life. Before he left, I went to my grandmother's house to see him off, and he gave me a small transistor radio in a black velvet case and some batteries. I cried endlessly. "Don't go, Daddy!" I don't know why I said those words because, at the time, it felt like I hardly knew my father. I suppose those tears were also an act of love. On my walk back home from my grandmother's house on Church Street to my mother's house on Bridge Street, I lost the batteries to the radio he had given me. It couldn't have taken me more than ten minutes to make that journey, but it seemed like forever. I never used that small radio, and I did not see my father again for several years.

My summers were not always filled with book reports. My mother ensured my siblings and I had some measure of fun as well. She planned a beach party for us at least one Saturday every summer, and we got to spend the entire day at the beach. She made sure to pack Maltas, soft drinks, and Palau, a rice dish with brown stewed chicken and one of my favorite meals, which she made especially for this occasion.

We also travelled to the countryside to spend days with a family friend. He was an older man who was a farmer. It seemed like we traveled for hours, usually in the back of a pickup truck or van, to get there. I can still feel the crisp Caribbean breeze rushing across my face and smell the fresh dew on the leaves. My siblings and I spent hours swimming in the cool river and catching crayfish, eels, and fish. We ate mangoes and a plethora of fruits unique to the Caribbean, and we cooked the day's catch on a fire started with dried banana palms between large rocks. After a long day, we made the trip back home to our village, exhausted, full, and content.

My mother was a strong, independent woman who, like her parents, owned her own shop. My earliest memories of my mother are of her working, and her career as an entrepreneur had several iterations. Some years, she would fly to America to purchase goods and return home to sell them in her shop. She always sold sweets, homemade cakes, and other baked goods, and she got up at the earliest hours of the day to bake and prep. These were gifts she had learned from her mother as a young girl. My mother loved her children and made immeasurable sacrifices for us all. I sometimes wonder how she was able to run a small business, raise three children alone, sing in the church choir, take care of her aging parents, and still manage to always look good doing it.

My mother taught me the real meaning of work ethic. She expected a level of excellence from me in a way that most Island mothers do. She inspired me to work hard at school, and when I excelled, she let me know how proud I had made her. Whether I had written an essay my teacher raved about or I had represented my entire school at a competition, it all made her proud. This propelled me to chase success and achievement from a very young age.

All my life, I have tried to model my mother's spirit of generosity. She was generous with her home and welcomed other family members to stay with us. Whether they were visiting from London or another part of the island, they were all welcomed. Often, we had to give up our own rooms to accommodate them. She prepared a delicious spread for guests and ensured our home was clean and hospitable. I suppose I also inherited my talent for entertaining from her.

As a child, I admired my mother for her grace under pressure. Her independence and her drive to succeed were much like a quiet storm—unfettered and profound. She embodied ambition and hard work. Looking back now, I understand how her character shaped my own sense of drive and ambition. I always wanted to be the first in my class in academics or otherwise, and I didn't have to work very hard at it. Learning came naturally to me. Several of my teachers and principals often reminded me how great a student I was and how much they appreciated having me in class. My teachers were such a positive influence in my life that I decided I, too, would become a teacher. As I advanced in grades, I placed an immense amount of pressure on myself to perform even better than I had the year before. I had to be number one, always.

I took home so many awards and competitions in my primary school career. However, the greatest achievement of my primary school tenure happened on the day my principal called our house to inform my mother that not only had I passed my Common Entrance Exam, but I had also achieved the highest grade in our entire school. My mother handed me our sage green rotary phone, and I heard my principal's voice on the other end, congratulating me. I burst into tears and fell on the bed, crying. It was a cry of relief and release. It was as if I was in a pressure chamber and the valve had suddenly been turned clockwise to release some of the pressure.

The Common Entrance Exams determine the high school future of every child born in the islands. I was twelve years old, and studying for this exam was perhaps the hardest I had ever worked up to that point. My teacher gave us extra lessons after school well into the evening hours to prepare, and on Saturdays, we returned to the school for even more math lessons. It was a cycle of never-ending studying, an academic boot camp. We were all anxious and terrified in the weeks leading up to the exam.

On the day of the exam, we traveled by bus to a local high school with lunchboxes packed with food clutched in our sweaty palms. I had studied, cried, and prayed. I visualized myself as a fighter stepping into a ring, ready to take on the fight of my life. At the time, it was my single greatest ambition to pass my exams and get accepted into St. Joseph's Convent, an all-girls convent school in the capital city of Castries. It was one of the best schools on the island, and my sister had already graduated from there.

The exams lasted all day. It was like being held captive, and each component of the exams held a coveted clue or key that brought me one step closer to freedom. We went from mathematics to English, to general knowledge, and then composition, and on and on it seemed to go. After it was over, I felt as light as a butterfly that had finally wiggled its dainty body out of a cocoon. I knew I had done well because I was prepared, but hearing my principal say the words, "You are going to St. Joseph's Convent," weeks later was truly a dream come true.

CHAPTER 2

STRANDED ON AN ISLAND

"HALLOWED WALLS WHERE OUR childhood unfolded its bright days." This was the beginning of our school anthem, which we sang during our morning assembly when I finally arrived at St. Joseph's Convent. I had been reminded ad nauseum that our principal, a nun named Sister Claire, was extremely strict. She would not hesitate to use Tickler, her leather belt, if the girls got out of line. As I walked up to the top of the hill on my first day of school—in my bright blue uniform, crisp white shirt, white shoes, and white socks, which had to be pulled up around my calves at all times—I felt the weight of the journey I was about to take.

I was not just a high school student; I was also a Convent girl. I would be following in the elite footsteps of generations of Convent girls who had gone before me — high-achieving women who had climbed the ranks of medicine, government, and academia. One of my new teachers, Ms. Laurent, had also attended St. Joseph's Convent several years before me. She did not hesitate to remind me that only excellence would be allowed of me once I walked through those doors. It was a daunting task and I felt intimidated. I was determined to be the best, as I always had been, but I soon learned I was among some of the most intelligent girls on the island, and I would have to work extremely hard to remain at the top.

As Convent girls, a lot was expected of us. The curriculum was rigorous and demanding. We were expected to always follow a strict code of conduct and represent the school to a standard that seemed impossible at the time. I continued to excel academically but had to work twice as hard as I had in primary school to achieve good grades. It was a different playing field, and because the school was located in the city, I had to take a bus from my village at an ungodly hour to get there. The journey seemed so long back then when I was twelve. After a night spent trying to finish copious amounts of homework for geography, English A or English B, Spanish, French, mathematics, integrated science, or religion, my mother would get me up at five o'clock in the morning to get ready for school. Every morning, a cold shower smacked me awake. If I missed the bus, which left at 6:30, I would never make it on time for morning assembly, and being late was simply not an option. It was unending and challenging to say the least.

My first year of high school, I found my closest friends, Shanasse and Lervan, who have remained my friends for more than twenty years. By this time, I had moved on from my goal of becoming a teacher—having discovered that teachers in St. Lucia were underpaid—and decided to become a doctor. Shanasse and Lervan also wanted to become doctors and we often discussed our dream of coming back to St. Lucia to start our own clinic one day. As often happens as we grow older, some of our life plans would shift. Shanasse would go on to become a nurse practitioner, and Lervan would pursue a PhD in education.

High school was filled with tears, sweat, and sacrifice. St. Joseph's Convent had all the characteristics of a girls' boarding school, minus the dorms. Our school was situated on top of a hill surrounded by bush, and a fence surrounded the compound. We were not allowed to leave the premises under any circumstance unless we had permission, and Ringo the dog's kennel was situated near the only defective gate in the back of the school to see to it we did not sneak out. Still, the bravest amongst us would sometimes slip out at lunch to buy chicken patties, beef patties, tamarind balls, orange juice, and lemonade from a vendor selling out of her home near the school.

Our lunch tables were more than where we sat to have a meal. They were where friendships were cemented, where we poured our hearts out to each other about whatever burdened us. Some of us brought packaged juice that came with individual straws for lunch. The rest of us squeezed limes, sour oranges, or grapefruits the night before, added water and sugar, and placed our juice in a reusable container to freeze so we could have a nice icy-cold drink at lunchtime.

My village was known for baking local bread from our traditional clay ovens, which the village bakers owned, and I often brought in local bread with butter or cheese and luncheon meat to share with my friends. Some of my classmates came with sliced bread cut into neat sandwiches with turkey, ham, or peanut butter. Some of them even brought pepper steak and rice, but I did not have steak for the first time until I immigrated to America. There was enthusiastic chatter about music videos seen on MTV and BET from those who had cable television. The rest of us listened because we only had access to two channels, HTS and DBS, and very often, the connection was so poor that even those two news channels didn't work. Instead of cable, we had outdoor antennas. One person often had to go outside and turn the antenna while another person stayed near the television to let the person outside know when to stop turning. You'd often hear: "Turn it. Turn it. Turn it. Okay. Right there."

Home economics was perhaps one of our most enjoyable classes as it was the least stressful. We worked in groups, and when we cooked, each person was responsible for purchasing some of the ingredients for the recipe. In our first year of high school, music was a mandated course, and we were all expected to learn to play the recorder. Students from primary schools in the city entered first form already knowing how to read music and how to play the recorder. Most of us from rural communities, however, had not been exposed to music theory in primary school. I witnessed a friend so petrified of our music teacher that she trembled with fear, making it impossible to keep her fingers on the correct holes of the recorder. The teacher berated her until she reached the point of tears.

I didn't know it at the time, but everything we were exposed to at St. Joseph's Convent was intentional and perfectly aligned with our greater purpose in this world. Every lesson learned was for our own refinement, including the lessons in session, a weekly class with Sister Claire. We lined up single file outside the audio-visual room, the only carpeted room in our school, took off our shoes, and awaited inspection as if we were soldiers in formation. If our socks were not on our shins, we were either scolded or smacked on the legs. If our nails were too long, she used a pair of scissors to trim them, and calcium spots on the nails resulted in three lashes on the knuckles with a ruler. "Drink. More. Milk!" After inspection, we sat in neat rows with proper posture and were taught life skills that would further define, redefine, and distinguish us as Convent girls.

Then there was elocution. Each class was assigned a poem to memorize and recite on Elocution Day on the stage of a large hall. One year, our class was assigned "Death Be Not Proud," by John Donne, and we made the grave mistake of not preparing for Elocution Day. To add insult to injury, some brave souls, who stood in the back and who had not memorized the poem, stuck a copy of the poem on the back of the person in the front of them. An example was made of us that day as Sister Claire berated our class in the presence of the entire school. We were then charged with the responsibility of not only preparing properly and performing our recitation again but also apologizing to the entire school.

The first time I heard the word "ostracized" was in reference to one of our schoolmates. She was ostracized for breaking a school rule. For a girl to be ostracized, she had to commit what the school considered grave sins at the time, like bringing alcohol to school. It was a strict Catholic school, and convent girls were expected to uphold the highest of standards at all times. Rather than wear her blue-and-white uniform, an ostracized girl was required to wear all white, much like a scarlet letter, and no one was allowed to communicate with her. If the threat of this punishment did not prepare us to become upstanding citizens, I don't know what would have. We were to become citizens who followed the rules and contributed to our society no matter where in the world we eventually migrated to.

Our teachers were passionate about teaching and would not hesitate to send us to the principal's office for the slightest infraction. Once, my English teach threw a chalkboard eraser at me because I dared to turn around to speak to a friend who sat behind me. It hit me square on my forehead. There was chalk dust all over my blue uniform and my face. I apologized to her for not following the rules and kept my eyes firmly on the blackboard for the rest of the class.

The literature we were exposed to allowed us to view the world through multiple lenses. Works like Shakespeare's *Macbeth*, *The Tempest*, and *Twelfth Night* moistened our palate as we prepared to dissect texts with varying levels of rigor. We were introduced to Langston Hughes and even dabbled in Robert Bolt's *A Man for All Seasons*. We read works by V.S. Naipaul and our very own Noble Laureate, Derek Walcott, for there was no summit when it came to academic engagement. At twelve, thirteen, and fourteen years old, the expectation was for us to become lifelong learners dedicated to becoming global citizens. The values and skills instilled in us through these experiences would remain indelible for years to come.

On September 10, 1994, exactly five days after I began high school, Tropical Storm Debby hit our island like a thief in the night. The rain began Friday evening, but most people did not heed the warnings urging those living in low-lying areas to evacuate. I woke up to the sound of a man banging on our front door, yelling for us to wake up because the water was rising quickly. He kept repeating, "Water! Water! Water!" in Creole.

My mother got us up in a panic. The water had already seeped under the doors and entered our house. It rose quickly, and soon, almost everything we owned in that home was engulfed by a brown, unrelenting wave. There was no distinction between the ocean and land in our village as the powerful waves from the flash flooding mimicked the waves of the ocean. It was like the ocean had appeared suddenly and swallowed the only world I knew.

The sheer force of the water made it impossible to unlock and open the front door to our house. My mother quickly opened a window and yelled for us to escape through it. The open window that served as our escape route would be the very same window through which all our buoyant possessions drifted into the unknown. I could not swim then, and still do not know how to, but somehow on that fateful day, I jumped from the window headfirst into the coldest water I had ever felt. It was so deep that it covered my head when I tried to stand. I am still unsure how I made it from our narrow yard onto the main street. I believe some men from the village grabbed my arms and eventually carried me to safety. Some of the older villagers were rescued with fishing boats. It was terrifying, and I now realize surviving a natural disaster of that magnitude is, in itself, a form of trauma.

I had lost almost everything—my new books, school uniforms, and clothes. Whatever remained in our house was covered in a thick layer of mud with a pungent earthy smell. We spent days sitting near the river after the storm, washing whatever we were able to salvage, until my wrists were slit from the endless friction brought about from rubbing the clothes to get the mud out. Relief in the form of food and clothing came through the Red Cross. Designated representatives for each village or constituency came by to distribute clothing and food for all those affected by the storm. We survived on packaged food items, such as crackers, tuna fish, corned beef, and sardines, for weeks. We ate whatever was available as choices were limited.

We stayed with my aunt and grandmother, my dad's mother, for several days after the storm. Then, my mother sent me to live with my uncle and his family in another part of the island so my education would not be interrupted. My brother went to live with another family in the city so he would be closer to his high school. My older sister and mother remained in our village to deal with the aftermath. I was homesick and dreaded heading back to my high school and reliving the trauma by telling the story. Some of my classmates who also lived in smaller villages outside the city were equally affected by the storm.

My principal, Sister Claire, called me into her office over the school intercom a week later. She was an intimidating woman, and I was nervous. When I got to her office, she told me she was aware my family had suffered a great loss, and she gave me several new uniforms, socks, shirts, and other school supplies. I felt a sense of relief because, for the first time, someone had asked how I was really doing and had affirmed me. Sister Claire didn't seem so petrifying in that moment.

The storm severely affected most of the island. Heavy rainfall and thunderstorms lasted over a six-hour period, which created massive landslides and immense flooding. There were countless injuries and four reported deaths as a result of the landslides. Roads and bridges were destroyed across the island. Farmers lost most of their crops, especially on the banana plantations. Parts of our hospitals and international airport also suffered damaged. It was reported that our island suffered EC$250 million in damages, which would have been roughly US$103 million at the time. It would be months before we returned to any semblance of normalcy in our homes. My mother's shop and our home survived the flooding, but it would take weeks to remove the debris that remained.

In my first year of high school, I got my first of many merit badges. They were awarded to students in each class who achieved the highest grades on the end-of-year exams. First-place, second-place, and third-place badges were announced at a ceremony each year. In my final semester of my first year of high school, I got the first-place badge. After all I had lost in the storm, I'd still managed to excel academically. I had never seen my mother so happy as when I brought my report book home. What remained after the storm, for me, was the will to succeed; the desire for excellence in all things has never left me.

During my first year of high school, I started a small business. Every week, my mother gave me toys and snacks from her store, and I carried them in my bag and sold them to my classmates. I was stunned that, each day, I sold every piece before the day was over. These were things the girls in my class could find in stores in the city, so why were they purchasing them from me? When we began learning to sew and embroider, I told my mom some of the girls didn't have sewing kits. She bought them, and I sold several small sewing kits that week. I realized the girls were paying for the convenience of having someone else source the items they needed for them.

I suppose I have always had an entrepreneurial spirit, and I kept the business going until, one day, one of my teachers found out and told me this was not allowed, and I could not conduct business in class. I told my mom I had gotten in trouble and could no longer sell to my classmates. I never found out who reported me, but it was a relief to no longer have to hide sewing kits and candy in my bookbag.

My other passion, which I enjoyed on the weekends, was singing with a chorale group and in the church choir. I spent hours in choir practice. We sang at hotels, especially during the Christmas holidays, and cultural events all over the island. We also performed at the Caribbean Festival of Arts, known as CARIFESTA, in Trinidad and Tobago one year. Perhaps the most profound performance I participated in was an Independence Day celebration. Our guest of honor was Nelson Mandela, and I still recall my level of excitement. I was nervous to even be in his presence. After we performed, he would not allow us to leave the stage until he shook everyone's hand. I was in awe of him and vowed to never wash my hand again. I don't recall what I actually said when it was my turn to meet him, but I do recall smiling from ear to ear.

When I was fourteen, during my second year of high school, my principal, Sister Claire, called me into her office again one day. Of course, my immediate thought was "What did I do now?" She told me our new physical education teacher, Ms. Hugh, wanted to meet me. She was from America, Caucasian, and worked with the Peace Corps. I needed to have eye surgery, and Ms. Hugh told me the Peace Corps would pay for all the expenses. She came to visit me at home one day and met my entire family. She was the kindest woman I had ever met. Everything happened so quickly, and within weeks, I had the surgery. I missed several weeks of school, but my friends came to visit me one Saturday during my recovery process.

Ms. Hugh not only became a family friend, but she also became my first mentor. I shared with her my desire to become a doctor, and she encouraged me in my studies and advised me to dream big dreams. She reminded me it did not matter what my current circumstances looked like and that I was more than capable of creating the life I envisioned. Even after her assignment to St. Lucia ended, she kept in touch all the way from America. When I returned to school, I knew I would need to work even harder to finish the school year strong.

In my third year of high school, I experienced the greatest loss of my life. That summer, my grandfather passed away. I was fifteen, and it felt like my world would collapse and I would be buried under the rubble. He was the first man to ever love me, and he was gone. I miss him today like I missed him on the day he died. When I got the phone call from my uncle saying my grandfather had died, I was devastated that I wasn't with him when he passed, and I fell to the ground, screaming in pain. It was my first true experience of grief because I had been so much younger when my grandmother died.

I have carried my grandfather with me on my life's journey. His generosity of spirit, his kindness, his incredible work ethic—everything I have accomplished in this life—I owe to him and his immense love for me. My sincere hope is that everyone will experience this measure of love in their lifetime.

My grandfather's death brought other changes to my life. That fall, my mother told me I would have to go live with a new family in the city because they lived close to my high school and I could walk to school. My mother's first cousin was a teacher, and she lived with her mother in a beautiful house within walking distance of my school. There was only one problem. I had never met them, and I did not want to leave home to live elsewhere yet again. However, I had no choice. I cried on my way there and prayed God would create some natural disaster so I would not have to go.

I lived with that family for an entire year. They were much older women, and there were no kids my age in the area I could get to know. After school, I spent hours in my room alone. I rarely spoke to my relatives, and I don't recall them speaking to me much either. We just didn't know each other. I was grateful they allowed me to live with them and tried to be the perfect houseguest as much as I could—always polite and helpful—but I missed my mother, my siblings, my village, and my life as I knew it. I looked forward to the weekends I got to go back home to my village, and I experienced deep separation anxiety every Monday morning when I had to return to the city.

High school became more demanding academically, and it didn't help that I was homesick. Then, the summer before I started my fourth year, my mother told us she would be moving to St. Thomas because my aunt had an emergency and my mother needed to assist her. My mother said I would have to live with my uncle, his wife, and their three sons while she was gone. She said it would be easier for me to get to school because my uncle had a car and could drive me.

I must have asked my mother a thousand times to let me stay in our home with my older sister while she was gone, but she refused. I cried because, in my young mind, my mother was leaving for good, but she assured me she would only be gone until January. I would not see my mother again for a decade.

I lived with my uncle and his family for a year. Hardly any of my friends at school knew I was no longer living at home or that my mother had moved to another island. I may have told one of my teachers and one of my closest friends, Natalie, but no one else. Even while I grieved my mother's absence, I continued to push myself academically. My mother sent me clothes and other gifts whenever she could, and I spoke to her on the phone often. Sometimes I cried when I said goodbye to her.

As the years went by, I learned to live with the distance between us. I know my mother loved me dearly and she probably did what she thought was best at the time. I did not understand the immense sacrifice she had made until I was in my thirties. The pain of separation I'd felt as a teenager was likely one thousand times worse for her as a mother. She was living in a brand-new country without her children, working hard, and building a new life. Alone in that foreign land, my mother must have cried many nights.

I can only imagine what her experience must have been like. For so many years, I saw this time of my life through the lens of abandonment and pain. As an adult, I now know the sacrifice she made was an act of love. For the lessons this has taught me and the woman it has allowed me to become, I will be forever grateful.

In my fifth and final year of high school, which is perhaps the hardest year for every high school student in the Caribbean, I moved one final time. This time, I went to live with another uncle and his wife and son. I loved living with Aunty Margo and Uncle Regis. I truly felt like I was part of the family and I could tell Aunty Margo anything, and they lived a bit closer to the city, so it took less time to get to my school by bus. I was thankful they provided me with an environment conducive to studying because this was the year I had to take my Caribbean Examinations Council (CXC) exams. Every high school student across the Caribbean had to take these exams to advance into our colleges or universities. For me, it meant I would attend Sir Arthur Lewis Community College to obtain my A-levels, which is an advanced degree. I needed to pass eight exams with very high scores: mathematics, English A, English literature, chemistry, physics, biology, French, and Spanish.

As the pressure of preparing for the CXC exams began to build, I experienced intense headaches, which lasted for days. I went to bed with them and woke up with them. I saw several doctors with little relief, but I pressed on. I worked hard and did what I do best—focused and pushed myself to the finish line.

The exams took place over a two-week period. My science classes also required that we complete labs and keep meticulous notes in our lab notebooks, which were also graded. The foreign language exams were separated into oral and written exams. Both English exams required us to write multiple essays. The English literature exam required that we recall specific books we'd read in the final two years of high school and answer essay questions on each one. I do not know how we were able to retain such a large volume of information.

That summer, I received my results and had passed everything. I breathed a sigh of relief. I had done the one thing I'd set out to do: get through high school and excel at my final exams despite all the challenges I faced on my journey.

Ms. Hugh returned to St. Lucia to visit that summer and took me to lunch. Then we went shopping for my prom dress. We talked about my plans for after high school, and I told her there was a possibility I would be moving to America to live with my dad and to attend university. I told her I still wanted to be a doctor, but I was anxious about what to expect in America. Ms. Hugh said, "Kama, you will do great in America. When you do start college, you will need to take it one day at a time. Focus on one class, one semester, one year at a time." I have taken this advice with me throughout my life.

At some point, Ms. Hugh and I lost touch, but I have always thought about her and wondered what she would think of my achievements so far. I call her my first Godwink, a term I learned from one of my mentors that was popularized by Squire Rushnell in his 2003 book *When God Winks*. She was the first of many people he would send to remind me I am seen and I am known by him—that all my needs will always be met, and no matter the circumstance, he will send someone to provide me with exactly what my heart desires at the time.

In the summer of 1999, I had to make one of the biggest decisions of my life—whether I should move to America or stay and attend Community College in St. Lucia. I labored over this decision. Either way, my whole life would change. I was seventeen years old.

CHAPTER 3

COMING TO AMERICA

O N AN EARLY SEPTEMBER morning, I boarded a flight from St. Lucia with my Aunt Margo. She was moving to Milwaukee to live with another one of my aunts, Aunty Rell, who had moved there years earlier. My final destination would be Miami, Florida. Aunt Margo and I said goodbye in Puerto Rico, and I made my way to my next gate alone. The summer before I moved to the US, I knew my life would change in a dramatic way and new opportunities were awaiting me in America. I was leaving so much behind, including my closest friends from high school, and I said goodbye to Abner, a friend with whom I had a lot in common. Her mother had moved to London shortly after my own mother left, and we'd supported each other through a lot during my final summer at home.

Abner and I cried together at the airport because I knew it would probably be years before I saw her again. I also said goodbye to the first guy I'd ever dated. I was seventeen, and my heart was breaking. I was leaving behind the only life I had ever known, and I felt the weight of that moment as I walked up the stairs of the airplane. The emotions I felt while on that flight were wide ranging. I experienced a sense of deep trepidation because I was going to live with my dad and his wife—and my brother, who had moved from St. Lucia one year before I did. I didn't know my dad or his wife very well. I was nine when he left St. Lucia, and we only spoke on the phone periodically, but he'd promised that if I moved to America, he would help fund my education. My dad knew my educational goals drove me more than anything else, and if nothing else would get me to move from St. Lucia, my dreams of becoming a doctor would.

There are countless reasons why people immigrate. To say goodbye to your life, your country, your loved ones and start again in a foreign land is, in itself, an act of faith and courage. Some people are chasing dreams they believe may be impossible to achieve in their birth countries. Others are running from poverty, famine, persecution, and civil wars. No matter what the reasons are, for all of us, it is a sacrifice and we pay a heavy price.

The sensory overload at Miami International was overwhelming. There were hundreds of faces, flights, gates being announced, and porters pleading to take my bags off the carousel and to the curb. My goal was to find my bags and then my father, but it felt like I was waiting for hours and I still could not find my dad. The day before I'd left for America, I'd visited my aunt, my dad's sister, to say goodbye. It had been an emotional visit, and she'd given me one hundred US dollars in case I had an emergency or was hungry at the airport. Now, I used the money she'd given me, bought something from a vendor to make change, and found a payphone.

I had my dad's work number in a small notebook I was carrying. I called the number and a voice announced, "Thanks for calling City Furniture." I asked to speak to my father but was secretly hoping he wouldn't be there and that he was somewhere in the airport looking for me too. However, he answered and said he was stuck at work but would be leaving shortly. I waited a few more hours until he arrived at the airport and found me. I was exhausted and hungry and was beginning to regret leaving St. Lucia altogether.

My first few months in Florida were filled with fear of the unknown and adjusting to the culture shock of being in a new community. We lived in an apartment building with hundreds of apartments, but I hardly ever saw our neighbors. I knew people lived there because there were always cars in the parking lot, but I do not recall meeting a single neighbor. Everyone seemed to be busy getting into or out of their cars. There was so much to take in, and the food was different from what I was used to back home. One evening, my dad took me to the McDonald's drive-thru to get a Big Mac, and I hated it. I couldn't finish it, and I have never eaten another one.

I stared at people as they drove by in their cars, but my dad said, "In America, you do not stare. It can be dangerous." I had to learn so many nuances about living in America, and I didn't enjoy spending countless hours in the apartment alone while my dad, brother, and stepmother went to work. I tried to fill my days with reading, journaling, and watching American TV, but I got bored quickly and became despondent. This wasn't how I'd imagined my American dream unfolding. I became depressed and spent many nights crying myself to sleep because I was so lonely and unhappy. I longed for St. Lucia; I missed home every day and I sometimes carried it like a heavy weight.

The silver lining to being in America was that I could use the power of the Internet to find friends who had moved away. One of my closest friends had moved to New York City in our third year of high school, and I was able to find her by sending an email. I was stunned when she responded. Now at least I had someone from

St. Lucia to whom I could vent. On weekends, I helped my dad's wife with her catering and decorating business. I also became a nanny for some of her friends' children. It paid very little money, but I was happy to do it because I could not spend another moment watching mindless TV. I needed something to do, and I was becoming desperate.

I frequently asked my dad about starting school. I daydreamed about being in school and imagined myself in class and making friends, and I even dared to imagine myself in a white coat. My dad said I would need to take the SATs, so I bought a book from the bookstore on SAT prep and took a class on Saturday mornings that helped me prepare. I studied every chance I got and took the exam a few weeks later. I also needed to transition from a tourist visa to a student visa. This turned out to be a long process, and I soon learned anything I needed to do through American immigration services would be lengthy, frustrating, and expensive.

While I missed home often and I longed for the day I could go back, my time in Florida also allowed me to grow in my faith. My dad's wife took me to Trinity Church with pastor Rick Wilkerson, in Miami Beach, every Sunday. This was such a different experience for me because I had always been a Catholic and had completed several sacraments in the Catholic faith before leaving St. Lucia. My experience at Trinity Church introduced me to faith in a tangible way. I experienced God for myself, and it was the beginning of a relationship that would provide me with comfort and a deep sense of peace through the toughest moments of my life. I learned it did not matter whether my time in America was unfolding in the ways I had imagined or not. I knew at my core that I was seen and known and that God would never leave me in a dark place forever. I began to realize there was a larger purpose for my life and it would find me in time.

Once I received my SAT scores and my student visa, I was finally able to apply to schools, and I decided on Florida International University (FIU) and their pre-med program. When I received my acceptance letter in the mail, I imagined my entire life would change and I'd finally be able to do the thing I came to America to do—get an education. I did not anticipate that I would need a way to get to school every day or that it would take hours if I tried to get there using public transportation.

After orientation, I enrolled in several pre-med courses and began my journey at FIU. During my first week of classes, I made a few friends. Some of them lived on campus and didn't have to worry about commuting, but I made one friend who told me she was also a commuter. Her parents were from Trinidad, but she had been born in Florida—and she had a car. She offered to pick me up in the mornings for class because she didn't live far from our apartment building. I was so grateful and knew this was another Godwink in my life.

My first week was intense—the science courses were rigorous, and my schedule was full—but one day, a man walked into my chemistry class and called out several names from a list he was holding. He said out loud to a room full of hundreds of students that those of us whose names he had called were to report to the bursar's office immediately to pay our bill. I'd heard him say Kama Thomas, but I pretended he wasn't speaking to me. I was mortified. If obtaining an education in America would be like this, I didn't think I would enjoy it very much.

After class, I went to the bursar's office and spoke with the woman behind the glass who told me, very matter-of-factly, I would need to pay more than five thousand dollars to the school for my classes for that semester. They would need to have this money before the end of the week, or I would not be allowed to continue to attend classes. She explained that my fees were more expensive because I was an international student. The cost took my breath away. I kept thinking, "Where will I find five thousand dollars in a week?" Then I remembered my dad had promised if I moved to America, he would help fund my education. I went home that evening, told my dad about the tuition and held my breath.

"I have no intention," my father said, "of paying for your education. Nobody owes you anything in this country."

"Then, what should I do?" I asked him.

"Kama, you will have to withdraw."

The next day, I went back to FIU and attended classes all day. Then I went to registration and explained I would need to withdraw from my classes because I could not afford the fees. I returned home that evening after a long day, locked myself in the tiny bathroom of our apartment, and cried on the floor until night fell.

I purposely left the lights off in the bathroom to match my mood. I was in despair. It felt like the room was closing in on me and there would be no joy in the morning. I was mourning the loss of a dream deferred. I was also coming to the realization that my father was incapable of honesty. At that moment, I knew I would need to rely on my faith and pivot into creating a new life for myself, a life in which I would not need to depend on anyone else to enable my dreams to come to fruition.

My father's wife moved back to St. Lucia almost a year after I immigrated to live with them. That year, my older sister moved to America to live with us as well, and that winter, she and I decided to take a bus to Milwaukee to visit my aunt and other family who had been living there for several years. We took a Greyhound bus. The trip was expected to take a little more than a day, but the bus broke down in Gary, Indiana, for several hours. It was extremely cold in Gary; there was snow everywhere, and I was ill-equipped for the extreme temperature. My coat wasn't warm enough, and I could not wait to get to our destination. After thirty-eight hours, we finally made it to Milwaukee. What was meant to be a few weeks' stay would last more than a year and a half.

CHAPTER 4

DELAY ISN'T DENIAL

MILWAUKEE ALWAYS SEEMED DREARY and cold. The snow never seemed to melt, and it felt like winter lasted for nine months. It was definitely not Florida. I wondered if the sun ever truly shone in Wisconsin. In Florida, I'd met people from almost every island in the Caribbean. On any given day, I heard Haitian Creole and Jamaican Patois, and I had even met some St. Lucians there. In Milwaukee, the only Island people I met were immediate or extended family. I thought it a very strange place. The silver lining was that my family lived there, which made it much more enjoyable.

I was determined to start school again, so my cousin and I enrolled at Milwaukee Area Technical College

(MATC), and I signed up for twelve credits of evening classes for my first semester. During the enrollment process, no one asked whether I was an international student; no one asked for a social security number. I held my breath while speaking to the admissions office and prayed they would never ask for any citizenship documents.

The cost of each credit was much more affordable than tuition at FIU. My mother helped with some of the cost for my classes, and I worked full time as a nanny to four children, ages three to ten, during the day. Each day, I rushed from my nanny duties in the suburbs, took a bus downtown, and hurried to evening classes. It didn't matter how exhausted I was. I was determined to never miss class. Every evening after school, I wrote papers, worked on college algebra, psychology, and sociology homework, and prepared for the next day. Most nights, I returned home at ten o'clock and studied until the early hours of the morning.

My saving grace was that academics had always come easy to me. While other students in my classes struggled with assignments, I excelled. During my college algebra class, we were asked to introduce ourselves, and I met an older woman who was also from St. Lucia. We were excited to meet each other, and she told me she also worked full time and she and her husband had been in America for several years. We studied together on weekends with her other friends, and I noticed they were all finding college algebra to be difficult. I couldn't understand why, but I helped them on weekends as much as I could.

One evening after class, my professor, an older woman from the Caribbean, said she needed to speak to me. I stayed back, wondering if I hadn't done well on our previous exam. However, that wasn't what she wanted to discuss. "Kama," she said, "I can tell this work comes naturally to you and you are very gifted, but I'm concerned that these older women you have been helping will hold you back." She encouraged me to keep my eyes on my bigger goal of medical school at all times.

By the second semester, the admissions office began to ask for a social security number to keep on file. I had to think fast, and I told the woman at the desk that I didn't know it. She told me, "You should know your social security number. You should have it memorized. Ask your mom when you get home." All I could get out was, "Okay." I didn't dare say I had no social security number or that I was currently living undocumented. I had been unable to renew my student visa after withdrawing from FIU because I was no longer a student. After that, I avoided the admissions office at all costs. My intention was to take as many credits as I could afford and remain in the shadows.

As a nanny, I made about five dollars per hour in cash. The days were long, and I remained in a constant state of exhaustion. One evening, the parents were late getting home, and I knew I would be late for class. I ran to the bus stop as quickly as I could, trying desperately to catch my breath, to make it downtown in time for class. Luckily, I made it on the bus.

"Ma'am, this is the last stop!" The bus driver's voice bolted me awake.

I looked around, and there was no one else on the bus. I had fallen into a deep sleep. I asked the driver, "How do I get back to MATC?"

"You'll need to walk back," he said, "This bus is now out of service."

I walked and walked until I found the school. I cried because I was cold, I cried because I was exhausted, and I cried because it seemed like it was always winter in Milwaukee.

An older man from St. Lucia, who was a family friend, told my older sister and me that we could make extra income by cleaning homes, so that's what we did. Many of my weekends were spent studying and cleaning other people's homes. One Saturday, we spent twelve hours cleaning the two-story home of an older Caucasian man in the suburbs. We got there at eight o'clock in the morning and were getting ready to leave around seven in the evening when he blurted out, "If you want to make some more money, you can clean out my office." When we were finally done at eight o'clock that night, he tried handing me a check for fifty dollars. He must have known we were undocumented and believed we had no rights to protect us.

"You are planning to pay both of us fifty dollars, right?" I asked him.

"No," he said. "You can split the fifty dollars."

I was livid. My older sister said, "Kama, let's just take the fifty dollars and get out of his house," but I refused. I looked him in the eyes and said, "No, you will pay each of us fifty dollars, or I am not leaving your house!" By this point, I was running out of patience with the man, and I was beyond the point of being rational.

He yelled at me, "If you don't take this check and leave my house, I'll throw you out in the snow!"

I walked towards him and yelled, "If you throw me in the snow, we will both end up in the snow tonight because I will lift you up and throw you in the snow too!" I was shaking, but I refused to back down from this fight. It was the principle. We had worked for hours with no break to clean his house, and he would pay us more than twenty-five dollars each. Deep down, this man knew what he was trying to do to us was illegal and morally wrong, but he knew we didn't have any papers and he was not going to rest until he took advantage of us.

My sister kept trying to get me to leave. I believe she was getting scared, but I didn't care. I wasn't leaving his house. Finally, his daughter came out of the kitchen and told her father he needed to write two checks, one to each of us. He did it begrudgingly and asked, "Whom do I make these checks out to?"

I had to think fast. I didn't have a bank account, so the check couldn't be in my name. I gave him my aunt's name, took the check from him, and walked outside so I could leave his house as quickly as possible. His daughter must have felt horrible because she offered to drive us home. As she drove, she apologized for her father's behavior. I told myself that night that, no matter what I needed to sacrifice to get an education in America, I would do it because I refused to spend my life threatening to throw people in the snow.

This was not our only experience with predatory customers. A few days before Thanksgiving, we cleaned the home of an older African American couple. Their children were coming to visit for the holiday, and the parents were excited. We cleaned all day, even cleaning the bar in their basement. We washed all their glasses and polished all their silver. At the end of the day, just as the Caucasian man had, they refused to pay us a fair wage.

I told myself, "I'll handle this one differently." Not all battles needed to be fought immediately; however, I intended to win the war. I took what the wife agreed to pay us and went home. Then I told my uncle what had transpired and gave him the phone number to the couple's house. My uncle called and told them, using some choice words, they had better bring us all the money we were owed or there would be consequences, and at six o'clock the next morning, there was a knock on the front door. It was the husband. He had stopped by to pay us more than we had asked.

That was the last home I cleaned.

A little more than a year after we moved to Milwaukee, my father called to say I'd finally received an interview with immigration and needed to return to Florida to continue the process to get a green card. I would miss living with my aunt and family in Milwaukee, but I was ready to finally find a path to living outside the shadows. For millions of immigrants, living in the shadows means continuously having to find unique ways to avoid admitting you don't have a social security number. Living in the shadows means people expect you to work long hours for little pay. It means constantly questioning whether your own dreams will ever come true. A life in the shadows is the heavy price we pay for our chance to achieve the American Dream.

The bright side of leaving Milwaukee to return to Florida was that I had completed twenty-three college credits, which I could transfer to a new school in Florida, and I had earned all As. There are some dreams which require we either find a way or make a way. I was determined to do both.

The immigration process was tedious. There were several steps, each of which required money. I showed up at the immigration office in Miami hours before my first appointment and found hundreds of people already waiting in line. At each appointment, the immigration officers seemed angry; they didn't smile much. Perhaps they were overworked. Or maybe their negative attitudes were meant to intimidate us. I was unsure of the reason, but even the security guards at the doors seemed miserable. It was as if they had all taken an oath to be curt and harsh.

I spent hours, over the course of several months, inside the stark walls of immigration offices. It was my least favorite place to be in America, until one day, after what seemed like an eternity, I was a green card holder! I hit the ground running, and I applied to and enrolled at Broward Community College. I transferred the twenty-three credits I had earned in Milwaukee, and after my first semester, I was inducted into the honor society. I took classes every semester and every summer without fail. I was going to run full speed ahead towards my finish line. Nothing could stand in my way.

I also interviewed at the Walmart closest to our apartment so I could walk to work. I started in the toy department right before Christmas, but after my first shift, my feet were sore. I came home in so much pain I didn't think I could return the next day, and I was determined to move out of the toy department. Within weeks, I applied to work at the register in the garden center, but that department is not conducive to human life during a Florida summer. Finally, there was an opening at the jewelry counter, and I applied. I did so well in my interview I was asked to start the following week.

Once I had a green card and a job, I could finally afford to pay for driving classes. I took my exam and passed on my first effort. I paid eight hundred dollars for a new engine for my father's old Toyota Tercel and could finally drive to school and work. I went to school full time during the day and worked full time in the evenings. I rushed from biology, chemistry, or calculus class to a three-hour lab and then rushed to work for an eight-hour shift. I usually headed home around ten o'clock at night to study or complete assignments, and then I did it all again the next day.

I just kept going. I don't remember ever missing a class. I showed up sick or tired because I was determined to never fall behind. When I read about the Walmart Higher Reach scholarship, I decided to apply. It required a certain grade point average, an essay, and community service. I already volunteered at BCC with the honor society, and my grades were great. I wrote the essay, submitted my application, and held my breath. One day, I walked to the back of the store to clock in, and there was my picture on the wall in the breakroom underneath the words "Higher Reach Scholarship Recipient." I had won! I hid in the bathroom and cried. The money would go directly to my school every semester to help offset the cost of my tuition. This was another Godwink.

One morning as I was preparing to leave for class, there was a knock on our apartment door, and my older sister answered it. It was a sheriff who told us we had twenty-four hours to vacate the premises because the rent had not been paid in several months. I left for school and spent the day feeling lost. I gave a presentation during my communications class, but I didn't hear any of the feedback my professor gave me. All I could think of was where I'd sleep that night.

I went to my classes, went to work, and then came home to pack all my belongings. I do not remember my father's explanation for why we were getting evicted, and it didn't matter. A few days later, my older sister, my brother and I moved into a condominium, where my brother and I split the rent every month. My father did not move in with us. Still, I didn't miss a day of class. I kept going. I told myself I would do whatever needed to be done to never again feel the uncertainty of not having a place to sleep. My mother would tell me years later she had been sending money to my father while we lived with him to help pay the rent, so she was deeply disappointed when she found out we were going to be evicted. I could only imagine what that must have felt like for her.

My goal was to graduate with honors, and I did. I worked on graduation day, but I received my associate's degree in the mail a few days later. Next, I set my sights on my bachelor's degree. That summer, I applied to transfer schools. I set my sights on Xavier University in Louisiana because I had read about their school of medicine and believed it would be the best fit for me. However, I spoke to Lervan, my friend from high school who was completing a post-baccalaureate program at Le Moyne College in Syracuse, New York, and she encouraged me to apply to

Le Moyne because of their small class sizes and excellent pre-med program.

I had never heard of Syracuse, and I was torn. I knew my time in Florida had come to an end and I was leaving to start the next phase of my life. I sold or donated what I could, including my car, and packed my bags. I resigned from Walmart and said goodbye to the friends I was leaving behind. But where I was going, Louisiana or Upstate New York, I wasn't sure. My little sister had moved to America to live with my dad and his partner a few months prior to my graduation, and her mom called and asked me to please take my sister with me wherever I decided to move to next. She preferred my sister live with me instead of our father. I was even more torn, but one August morning, my older sister, my little sister, and I boarded a flight to Syracuse.

CHAPTER 5

A NEW YORK STATE OF MIND

THE SUMMER WE LANDED in Syracuse, I had a lot to do in little time before the school year began. My sisters and I moved in with my friend Lervan, whom I had known since my high school years in St. Lucia. She lived in a one-bedroom basement apartment in an old building that seemed like it had not been repaired in a century. There were broken windows and strange smells in the staircase. I'm still unsure how we all fit into a one-bedroom, but we made it work.

Ready to enroll in classes as soon as possible so I wouldn't miss the first day of the semester, I went to the office of continuing education, where I met with a woman named Pat. She assisted me with the entire process of enrolling, and she would take me under her wing throughout my time at Le Moyne. She would take me to a store at the beginning of winter and buy me a proper winter jacket, which helped me get through the extreme Upstate New York winters. Looking back, I now know she was another Godwink on my journey.

My dad had provided me with a notarized letter stating I was the legal guardian for my sister, who was fourteen at the time. That first week in Syracuse, I made an appointment to enroll her in a local high school, the closest one to our apartment and the one Pat had recommended once she found out my sister was with me. I didn't yet realize the level of responsibility involved in being my younger sister's legal guardian. I never stopped to think about it. I just hit the ground running.

I enrolled in Le Moyne's pre-med program and started school that fall. My weeks were full of classes, labs, exams, and making sure my little sister was also succeeding at her new school. I went to parent-teacher conferences and meetings and made sure she wasn't having any issues in her classes. A few weeks after we moved to Syracuse, my older sister moved to New York City for a job.

Pat introduced me to her friend Maria, who was also a professor from Le Moyne, and Maria's partner Maryellen. My sister and I were invited to dinner one evening at Pat's, where we got to meet Maria and Maryellen's beautiful daughters. They had adopted the girls as infants, but they were about three and four years old when we met them. One of my favorite memories is doing the girls' hair on weekends. We ate many dinners and spent countless hours with Maria and her family. They would become one of my greatest Godwinks during my time in Syracuse.

Days after I started school at Le Moyne, Hurricane Katrina hit the city of New Orleans and displaced over one and a half million people, including students at Xavier. Had I decided on Xavier University, I would have lived through yet another natural disaster and probably would have been displaced again. There have been so many choices I've made in my life that I could not understand at the time, but years later, I realized they were truly for my highest good and God has remained with me every step of the way. My decision to move to Syracuse was one of them.

A few weeks after starting Le Moyne, I interviewed for a job at a restaurant supply store in downtown Syracuse and got the position. I would finish classes and take the bus downtown, work until the store closed, and then take the bus back to our basement apartment and study for long hours into the night. I needed to stay on top of my classes if I was to succeed at physics, organic chemistry, and cell and molecular biology. I had little time to hang out with the few friends I made.

There were very few black students in my classes, and I only encountered one black professor during my time at the college. His name was Dr. Makuja, and he taught my summer class on the Rwandan genocide. Dr. Makuja always made sure I had eaten lunch and was coping well with all my responsibilities. He encouraged me to keep going and to not lose track of my final goal of graduation. There were so many afternoons when I had no money for lunch, but I went to his office and he took me to the school cafeteria to pay for my meal. We have remained in touch in the years since.

One particularly cold winter morning after a heavy snow fall, I walked to the bus stop to wait on the bus to school. My first class was cell and molecular biology lab. We had a short quiz before each lab and we could not be one minute late. The snowbanks were so high that that morning, the bus driver must not have seen me standing there, and I chased the bus to no avail. Filled with anxiety that I would not be allowed to take the quiz, I walked to school. I was more than five minutes late, and my professor did not permit me to take the quiz.

Our classes were rarely canceled due to severe weather because most students lived on campus, and on days like that, I wished I could afford to live on campus too. However, I made sure I never missed another quiz. Walking through frigid Upstate New York winter weather would have to become my specialty.

Our basement apartment became increasingly difficult to live in. There were always strange characters walking in and out of the building, and the couple upstairs fought often and loudly. I usually stayed up studying into the early hours of the morning and found ways to not allow the noise from upstairs to distract me. I learned how to compartmentalize my life because graduation was the only thing on my mind.

To make matters worse, the basement flooded one day, which caused a terrible black mold problem. The landlord, a middle-aged white man, insisted we did not have a mold problem and refused to do anything about it. As the problem got worse, my health deteriorated. I often woke up lightheaded, dizzy, and with a headache that would not go away. I made several trips to the ER with nausea and vomiting. Nothing helped.

Maria and Maryellen came over one afternoon to talk to our landlord about the black mold issue. It was a heated discussion, but he finally allowed us to break our lease. My friend Lervan, my little sister, and I moved into a mold-free, two-bedroom apartment closer to Le Moyne College. Maria introduced us to some of her other friends: Hetty and her partner, Suzanne, Aunt Debbie, Grandpa Lionel and his wife, and so many other women who all became surrogate mothers to us. They brought so many things for our apartment: furniture, comforters, and household items we didn't know we needed. Many nights and weekends, they fed us. Hetty and Suzanne even provided me with a cell phone.

I owe so much to the women in Syracuse who showed up for us when we needed it most. I have never forgotten their kindness towards me and hope to always pay it forward in my own life. I have kept in touch with all these women and still call them when I need advice. I know they remain truly invested in my success.

With the apartment issue resolved, I got a second job as a biology tutor for Higher Education Opportunity Program (HEOP) students after meeting the assistant director of the program, Ms. Caine. She permitted me to work around my class and lab schedule and offered me as many hours as I could humanly work. I provided one-on-one tutoring for students who needed it and group tutoring sessions the nights before their biology exams. Some students showed up to every session with a list of questions, ready to work. Others complained, were never prepared, and went out of their way to cause a disturbance during my sessions. I had zero tolerance for them. If they only knew how long it had taken me to begin the process to obtain an education in America, they would appreciate theirs. If only they knew there were intelligent students all over the world who would give everything to get an education in America, that there were still countries where girls were not afforded any education. I showed up for the students who were committed to learning and asked the disrupters to leave.

I was walking on the quad, heading to the cafeteria, when a young black woman walked up to me, introduced herself as Kristin, and asked, "Do you like to sing? We're looking for voices to add to the gospel choir." I rolled my eyes. I did not have the time for this. I was working two jobs as a pre-med major and was also the legal guardian to a teenager. However, when she invited me to attend choir practice the next week, I realized I missed singing and had always felt at home and enjoyed a sense of community in a choir. A week later, I showed up to choir practice and a lifelong friendship with Kristin was formed.

When I wasn't tutoring freshman biology, I was locked in a study room in the library, studying for an exam, completing my notes in my lab book, or preparing for a presentation. I also worked on research with one of my professors a few days a week, and we spent hours in the lab. I noticed Kristin was never busy with schoolwork and she seemed to always have free time. So why was I always stressed and running from one class to the next? Kristin explained that she was a communications major and most of her assignments involved writing papers. We were having completely different college experiences. When we looked at our grades at the end of a semester, she wouldn't bat an eye if she ended up with a C in a class. Meanwhile, a C in any class would send me into a hemorrhagic shock.

Kristin never understood why I was so busy or why I spent such long hours in the library before every exam. One day she asked me, "Why must you push yourself to make the dean's list every single semester?"

"For years after landing in America," I told her, "I dreamed of what it would be like to get an education. To sit in a college class and study for exams. To learn new things. Do you know how many countries there are in the world where girls are still not allowed an education? It's a privilege for so many, a distant dream that they may never experience."

She looked on in silence, like she was hearing this information for the first time.

"I cannot waste this opportunity I have been given," I continued. "I am not going back to St. Lucia unless I'm able to achieve what it is I came to America to do."

"Wow, Kama," Kristin said. "I never thought about it that way." For her, obtaining an education seemed burdensome, like something that got in the way of her other daily activities. She finally realized that, for me, it was a gift, an honor, and the thing I had left all the comforts of home to pursue. I had sacrificed a lot to walk through these halls, so even the most stressful days were worth it.

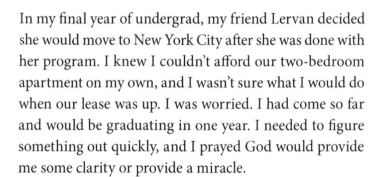

In my final year of undergrad, my friend Lervan decided she would move to New York City after she was done with her program. I knew I couldn't afford our two-bedroom apartment on my own, and I wasn't sure what I would do when our lease was up. I was worried. I had come so far and would be graduating in one year. I needed to figure something out quickly, and I prayed God would provide me some clarity or provide a miracle.

One evening, while I was eating another dinner with Maria and her family, I told them Lervan was leaving, and I would need to find an apartment I could afford for my sister and me. Maria told me my sister and I could move in with her, Maryellen, and their two little girls. They truly had become like a family to me, but I didn't expect she would offer us a place to stay. She hardly knew us. I was stunned, but I thought maybe this was the miracle I had prayed for. I told her I would think about it. I was unsure and didn't want to make the wrong decision, but I had run out of options.

A few weeks later, my sister and I moved in with Maria and her family. It was a challenging time for us all. Maria was a therapist, and I was an introvert who hardly spoke and craved alone time to maintain my peace. I had always required time alone. I was not used to being in a family where I was asked to talk about my feelings. It was so new to me, and I was overwhelmed. I'm sure it was not an easy time for my little sister either.

Although there were difficult moments, there were also many beautiful moments, which I have carried with me through the years. Maria and Maryellen's children became my little sisters. I was protective of them and loved them like I had known them all my life. Over the years, when I have gone back to visit them, it has always been like no time has passed. The girls are still my little sisters and that will never change.

I learned so much during my year with Maria and her family. I learned that sometimes a family can be the people we choose or the people who choose us—not necessarily the people we are related to. I learned love is a verb, an action. I learned there are people who require nothing in exchange for their kindness. I don't know what my final year in undergrad would have been like if Maria and Maryellen had not provided me with a safe harbor, a shelter, a place of rest, but I am grateful I didn't have to find out. I will never know why they agreed to allow us to live with them. I may never know the level of sacrifice or the cost to their family, but I do know I am still deeply grateful. They provided us with a sense of safety I hadn't experienced in several years. It allowed me to quit my job at the restaurant supply store and focus fully on my courses, and my sister was finally able to have her own room. Maria and her family gave me a year when I could finally breathe.

Finally, that May, I walked across the stage to accept my degree—and I graduated with honors. Some of my family and friends came from around the country to watch me accept my diploma. Although my mother was unable to attend, she told me how proud she was of me that morning on the phone. It was an emotional day. I wished my mother could have been there, but I knew she was there in spirit.

After graduation, I did something I had been hoping to do for a decade. I flew to St. Thomas to visit my mother.

It was an emotional reunion, especially since she didn't know I was coming. I stayed with my high school friend Shanasse and her husband on the island of St. Croix. I called my mom the day I landed on St. Croix to say I would be taking the seaplane to St. Thomas to visit her in two days. At first, she didn't believe me, but once she spoke to Shanasse, she realized I was really in the Virgin Islands. When I made it to St. Thomas, my mom was waiting for me as I got off the sea plane. It seemed like time stood still as we ran towards each other in the street. We cried and hugged for what seemed like hours. I hadn't seen her since I was fifteen, and I was now twenty-five years old.

The week I spent with my mother enabled me to see what her life had been like all those years. She worked at the only children's home on the island. I met the children she was responsible for caring for, the friends she had made, and her coworkers. We went to the beach, took a boat to St. John to visit the ruins, and shopped for souvenirs near the cruise ship ports. My mother knew I had missed her cooking, so she made all my favorite meals. The days went by quickly, and our goodbye at the airport was painful. I cried long and hard because I was unsure when I'd get to visit her again.

The summer after graduation, I accepted a sales job with AT&T, and my sister and I moved into a one-bedroom apartment that I could afford. I made very little money, but I made it work. My little sister needed to complete one more year of high school, so I had to remain in Syracuse until she graduated. It was a difficult year. I was working at a place I didn't enjoy. I had to become a parent figure to my sister, and our relationship suffered because of it. I prayed I was doing the very best I could, but I was overwhelmed and unfulfilled. I know now that it should never have been my responsibility to raise her while I was also trying to figure out the rest of my life.

That summer, I studied for the MCAT, the entrance exam for medical school, but when the day of the exam arrived, I made the difficult decision not to take it. I had studied for weeks but I didn't feel ready, and I was unsure whether this was a dream I still wanted to pursue. I called my friend Justin on the phone and told him I didn't know if this was what I was supposed to do with my life. I had worked towards that dream for so long that I never took any time over the years to re-evaluate whether it was something I wanted to continue pursuing. I had been in survival mode for so long, and I was exhausted.

Then I read about offshore US medical schools that would allow me to study in the Caribbean, and I thought they would be a perfect fit. I applied to the American University in Antigua and waited. A few weeks later, I received an email with information for an interview, and weeks after my interview, I received an acceptance letter. I paid the five-hundred-dollar down payment to secure my seat, but I decided to wait until the next year to attend so my sister could finish high school in Syracuse. The medical school informed me I could not defer my enrollment and would need to give up my seat if I wasn't planning to attend that fall. So I gave up my seat.

My little sister completed her final year of high school and decided on Columbia University in New York City for her undergraduate education. She told me she had gotten a full ride, and I was beyond proud of her. Her hard work and sacrifice had paid off. The night before the ceremony, she invited me to her graduation, but it was too late to take the time off work, so I couldn't attend. I got the sense she didn't really want me there or she would have told me weeks earlier.

A few weeks later, I came home from a draining day at work and found my sister had left a note on the table saying she had moved to New York to start college. I didn't see or hear from her again. Several years later, on a trip to the city, I saw her coming out of a subway and she pretended not to see me. We both kept walking. It took me years to realize I had done the best I could in that situation. I did not have the tools to be a parent to her, nor should I have been required to try. I released her in love and prayed for her success and safety.

My time in Syracuse had come to an end. I didn't know where the road would lead me, but I remained open. My friend Kristin had moved to the Washington, DC, metro area for a job at the Pentagon, and she suggested I move there for a change of scenery, which I definitely needed. In August 2009, I landed in DC, unsure of my next steps but ready to accept whatever challenges lay ahead.

Three months after moving to Northern Virginia, I interviewed for a job as a pharmacy technician with Walmart Pharmacy. My pharmacy manager was a young Vietnamese woman named Lien. She was excited for me to start and told me how impressed she'd been by my interview. I loved assisting patients and learning about the medications, and I quickly made new friends. I worked long and hard hours. Some days were extremely difficult because we not only worked quickly but also had to make sure we were accurate. The pay did not correspond to the level of work I was putting in every week, but I showed up every day with a renewed sense of purpose and felt I could truly make a difference in patients' lives.

Over lunch one day, Lien asked whether I had ever thought of going to pharmacy school. She knew I was thinking about reapplying to medical school and that I was becoming increasingly frustrated about not living up to my fullest potential. She said, "Kama, you are so good with patients. You would make a great pharmacist." She explained what her pharmacy experience had been like at Temple University, and she encouraged me to apply.

That evening, I went home to research schools of pharmacy, and I decided on Massachusetts College of Pharmacy in Boston. I prayed and told myself I would only apply to one school, and if I got accepted, then it was meant to be.

All the research suggested I apply to multiple schools to increase my chances of getting accepted, but I decided against it. I applied and then I waited.

I received an email for my interview a few weeks later. I prepared for several days, and Kristin agreed to fly to Boston with me. On interview day, I woke up early, prayed, and headed to the school. It was a long day that involved a tour of the campus and interviews with several faculty members. We were also tasked with writing an essay. My topic question was: "Do you believe that marijuana should be legalized? State your reasons for or against its legalization." The essay was timed, so I wrote feverishly. After a long day, I left Boston and headed back to Virginia, hoping I had done well and anxious to find out my fate.

I came home one day from an exhausting day at the pharmacy, and there was a large white envelope in the mail. I could not recall what I'd read on the internet. Was a large envelope an indication that I had been accepted? Or was it a small envelope? Finally, I opened the envelope. "Dear Kama Thomas, Congratulations on your acceptance..." I cried and cried some more.

There was so much to do to prepare for my move to Boston. I couldn't wait to get back to work to let Lien know I had gotten accepted. When I did, she expressed real joy at the news. I owed so much to her for believing in me, guiding me, and encouraging me along the journey. She was definitely another Godwink in my life.

I had always imagined myself in a white coat. I always knew my career would be in healthcare or medicine in some way but would never have guessed it was meant to be as a pharmacist. Growing up, I didn't know one pharmacist, but so much of my journey had led me to this exact moment in my life. I suppose pharmacy found me.

Looking back, I realize my work-life balance would have suffered had I gone to medical school, and I would have been miserable because I feel everything so deeply. But my family had supported me in my dream of becoming a doctor, and in that moment, I worried about what my mom would say when I told her I'd changed my mind. I had a conversation with her, and she assured me she would support me no matter what I decided to do with my life as long as I did it well. That freed me, and I let go of any concern or disappointment. Even though I was afraid, I felt a sense of peace that I had made the right decision.

The summer before I moved to Boston, the school informed me my acceptance was contingent on me completing three courses I had not taken in undergrad, microeconomics, macroeconomics, and Calculus 2. I had very little time to get this done, but I was determined. I enrolled in online courses at Northern Virginia Community College and pushed myself. As fate would have it, I was dating a guy, Arusha, who was also a math teacher. He was one of the kindest and most generous people I'd ever met, and he was a huge help while I tried to teach myself Calculus 2 online. Every day, I left work at the pharmacy to work on assignments, finish papers, and study for calculus exams, which I had to complete in person.

I met with my calculus professor and explained to her that I needed to pass this class in order to start pharmacy school and I needed whatever suggestions she had. She told me she admired my drive and I'd need to be diligent about studying the course material, especially since taking it online would be much more challenging than an in-person exam. Because of my work schedule, online classes were my only option at the time, but that summer I did what I do best. I kept my head down and worked hard. I finished all my classes and earned two As and a B in Calculus 2. I was going to Boston. Kristin got me a parting gift, a laptop for my classes, and that August, I landed at Logan International Airport with a small carry-on bag with a twin airbed folded inside.

CHAPTER 6

FROM WHITE COAT CEREMONY TO HOODING CEREMONY

I **LANDED IN BOSTON AFRAID** and alone. I knew no one in this city. My first order of business was to make my way from the airport, find my landlord to retrieve my keys, and then head to Adams Village, in Dorchester, to locate my studio apartment. Adams Village was a primarily Irish neighborhood, approximately an hour from Boston by train. After several bus and train rides, dragging my suitcase around the city, I finally found my apartment. It was unfurnished, so I blew up my airbed, called my mom to cry, and went to sleep. The next day, I made my way from Dorchester for orientation. I took a bus and two trains to get to class, and I knew the winter commute would be tough.

That weekend, Kristin and Arusha drove eight hours in a U-Haul from Virginia to deliver my bed and clothes. We went to Goodwill to purchase other furniture, including a desk and anything else I could fit in my studio apartment. I was so grateful.

I needed to make a friend in my class, and in bio-chemistry class, I kept searching for black faces in the sea of students in the large lecture hall. There must have been three hundred students in the room, but I don't believe I counted fifteen black students that day. I found a girl who looked serious but friendly, and I told myself I would sit near her and pray she spoke to me. I asked her where she was from, and she answered that she was from the Ivory Coast but was born in France. Her name was Fatima, and we talked about how nervous we were for biochemistry because we had heard how difficult it would be.

Fatima and I took the train home together. Her stop was downtown, but I changed to the red line to get to Dorchester. On the train ride, she told me she was one-fourth of a set of quadruplets. She had two sisters and one brother who'd all shared a womb with her. I knew we would be friends forever. She was my kind of person because I sensed she had a calm demeanor and we shared a lot of common interests. She talked about her Muslim faith and her family and how important both were to her.

"I promise to devote myself to a lifetime of service to others through the profession of pharmacy. In fulfilling this vow: I will consider the welfare of humanity and relief of suffering my primary concerns. I will apply my knowledge, experience, and skills to the best of my ability to assure optimal outcomes for my patients..."

Three hundred students stood inside a large lecture hall reciting the Oath of a Pharmacist out loud. Our white coating ceremony occurred nearly one month into the start of the PharmD program. We took the oath together, and one by one in single file, we walked to the front of the room and stood as our professors helped us put on our white coats. The gravity of the moment was not lost on me. I could feel the weight of the great responsibility being entrusted to us.

I was on the brink of tears but held them in. The white coating ceremony signified our entry into the profession. While I had once thought the white coat I'd dreamed of wearing would represent my career as a medical doctor, it turned out to represent a different purpose for my life that allowed me to do healing work in an unanticipated way. During the ceremony, we were reminded of those who went before us and paved the way for us to stand in this moment, and I thought about the patients I would meet and how I would impact their lives. I looked around at all the faces of my peers who would become fellow lab partners, group project companions, and those who would eventually become friends.

My first exam was in pharmaceutics. I studied for several hours after class and all weekend. When our results were posted, I logged on to see how I'd done. Seventy-six! I was stunned. I had studied, so there was no way this was my actual grade. I went to the professor's office to look through my Scantron answer sheet and review my wrong answers. I really did get a seventy-six on my first exam in pharmacy school. I went to the bathroom and cried in a stall. Every limiting belief played in my head. *Did I make the right choice coming here? Is this what I'm really meant to do? Maybe I'm not cut out for professional school.* I took the train home, defeated.

I gave myself two goals. One, I would make the dean's list at the end of that semester, and two, I would get inducted into the honor society before I graduated. I went home to my studio apartment in Dorchester and wrote my goals on a Post-it note. I also wrote Psalm 46:5 on a yellow sticky note and attached it to my bathroom mirror. *God is within her; she will not fail!*

It turned out that everyone was correct about biochemistry. It was the bane of my existence. It made no sense; it was like a foreign language. I went to tutoring sessions, I reviewed old exams, and I did not miss a class. Mostly, I worked hard.

The commute to and from Dorchester made my first year very difficult. I was exhausted from the train and bus rides and the late-night studying, but I was equally exhausted from the antics of my drunk neighbor who lived directly across the hall from me. He was an older Irish man who terrorized the building whenever he drank. I knew it was time to leave my apartment when he stole the keys to my door and yelled out loud, "I found your keys. Come and get them!"

I knocked on his door a few minutes later to retrieve my keys, but he walked out completely naked and said, "Sorry, I didn't see them."

I pretended he wasn't standing there naked. "I heard you yell out you had my keys, and I would like them back."

He insisted he didn't have them, and suddenly, I felt unsafe. I packed a bag and went downtown to stay with my friend Fatima. I just needed to get through the week, which was exam week. I did not renew my lease; my time in Dorchester had come to an end. Arusha flew to Boston after my exams and helped put all my stuff in storage before I left the city for the summer.

I returned to Virginia during every break to work as an intern at a Walmart pharmacy because I needed the money and the practice. There were so many people in Virginia who showed up for me during my pharmacy school years. They fed me, provided me a place to stay, and prayed me through. The Morgan family, my friend Yenni and her family, Lien Lee and my entire pharmacy family believed in me every step of the way. I completed my first of many required internships in Virginia during my first summer of pharmacy school.

At the end of my first year, I had made the dean's list both semesters—quite an improvement from a seventy-six on my first exam. I was in the right place, doing the right thing, and I had everything I needed to succeed. I refused to give up. I dismantled my limiting beliefs one by one. I had hit my stride.

After my summer internship, I returned to Boston to start my second year and moved into a new apartment near the university. I would share the space with two other girls from my class, who I didn't yet know, Chantal and Nadine. I couldn't find anyone besides Fatima to help move my stuff out of storage; Arusha couldn't come this time because of his work schedule. As we sat on the train headed towards the storage facility, I could tell Fatima was worried. How would we ever get my bed, a desk that weighed what seemed like a hundred pounds, books, and clothes out of the storage, onto a U-Haul, and then into my room? I had not thought this out well. When I opened the door to my storage unit, we sighed heavily.

Out of nowhere, I heard a man's voice yell, "Do you ladies need help?" Fatima and I answered unanimously, "Yes, yes, we do!" He was an older man from Haiti with a full white beard, and he introduced himself as Mr. Harry. He stayed with us the entire day and emptied out my storage unit, loaded everything into a U-Haul, drove it to my new apartment, and unloaded all my furniture.

We were turning our two-bedroom apartment into a three-bedroom because of the $1800 monthly rent. To save money, I converted the living room into my bedroom. There was no door, but Mr. Harry made me a makeshift door with thick curtains and a divider. Throughout the rest of my pharmacy school journey, Mr. Harry would make sure I had a ride to the grocery store and to job interviews, and he would feed me more times than I can recall. One winter, because of a major snowstorm, I couldn't get back to Boston from Virginia. I tried for several days and could not get on a flight. Mr. Harry recommended I take a bus to New York City so he could pick me up from there. He drove me from New York back to Boston, in the winter, so I wouldn't miss a day of class. He was my biggest Godwink thus far.

Often, I look back on the moments of my life when I felt strongly that something or someone outside of myself was looking out for my best interest. My time in Boston was the perfect example of this. I have often felt God is especially fond of me.

During my second year, I completed my first hospital internship at Virginia Hospital Center. My preceptor, Dr. Mireku, encouraged me to create my pharmacy rotation on my own terms. He encouraged me to dream big and allowed me to work with the hospital diabetes educator, Ms. Kay Tucker, as often as I wanted to. I learned so much from her, and she allowed me to work independently to build my confidence. I would return to Virginia Hospital Center during my final rotations in my fourth year, and Dr. Mireku would again allow me to create my own rotation, working with the diabetes educator the entire six weeks. It was one of the most profound experiences I had as a student.

While working with Kay Tucker, I started a performance improvement project at Virginia Hospital Center to improve blood sugars in admitted patients. During my last week of rotation, I was able to present my data and conclusions to the glycemic committee on my final day. Months later, I received an email from Ms. Tucker informing me that, as a result of my project findings, the hospital had implemented new workflows that positively impacted patients.

On April 15, 2013, Patriot's Day, I met my friend Kelly in the library to study for our final exams. She was an international student from Beijing, and we had become very good friends. It was Boston Marathon Day, and we had the day off from class, so I was determined to go watch the runners cross the finish line. I knew exactly where I wanted to stand to get the best view. After several minutes, I finally convinced Kelly to take a break from studying so we could take the train downtown.

We walked to the station and waited for the train to arrive, but we didn't board the train because Kelly felt strongly that we should not go to the finish line. She said we should head back to the library to study so we could "finish the year strong." We walked back to school, and an hour later, I received a call from Fatima. She sounded alarmed. "Kama, I'm stuck on the green line. Do not come downtown. A bomb went off at the marathon!" I couldn't believe what I was hearing. Around 2:49 p.m., two pressure-cooker bombs, which had been hidden in backpacks, exploded within seconds of each other near Boylston Street—right at the finish line. The bombings claimed the lives of three spectators and two hundred sixty people were reported injured.

The next five days in Boston were a blur, and a dark cloud fell over the city. It didn't feel like the same place I had grown to love. We were on lockdown for several days and were not allowed to leave our homes until the suspects were found. It was a difficult and emotional time. I walked into my professor's office a week after the bombings because I needed to speak to someone about the emotional pain I was in. I felt shaken.

Kelly told me a few days later that her friend from Boston University had gone to watch the runners cross the finish line and no one had heard from her since. Once all the names of the victims had been released, Kelly informed me that her suspicions had been correct and her friend, an international student from Beijing, had not survived.

We remained in a state of shock and grief for months. We attended vigils, and a service was held at school to honor the lives lost. We were provided with grief counselors and were encouraged to talk through our feelings, all while we tried to return to our usual class schedules, labs, and exams. We were all hurting. Kelly returned to Beijing after residency and we have lost touch, but I've always been grateful she didn't allow us to get on the train on that Patriot's Day.

In September 2013, I returned to Boston for my third and most difficult year of pharmacy school. Four months had passed since the bombings, and once again, I'd spent the summer working as a pharmacy intern in Virginia. My weeks were full of pharmacology, medicinal chemistry, labs, therapeutics, and hours upon hours of studying. Most weekends, I headed to the library at seven in the morning to study, and some days, I stayed for fifteen hours. It was lonely and draining. I studied, took exams, and then studied some more. This was my life for months on end. My stress level was high, constantly, but I leaned on my faith.

Boston winters were incredibly trying for me. It didn't matter how long I lived in America; I would never get used to the extremes in weather. That winter, while walking to the library for a long study session, I slipped on ice and landed loudly on my back. My lunch and my bag flew across the street. I heard a man's voice approaching me, asking loudly whether I was okay. He helped me up, and I kept walking towards the library. Everything hurt, but I ignored the pain and kept studying.

For an entire week after my fall, I had an intense migraine. Nothing helped. Finally, my primary care doctor recommended I try physical therapy. Even with the therapy, it would be several months before I felt better. I had seriously hurt my back, but somehow, I never missed a class or an exam.

I sang in the choir at the Catholic church near our apartment, and I volunteered as often as I could. I even made new friends in class. Donna and I bonded over our faith and love of good Korean food, and my roommates also became my lifelong friends. I refused to be consumed by the raging fire that was pharmacy school. Through the sweat and sacrifice, I excelled academically, and that year, I was inducted into Rho Chi, the pharmacy honor society. It was no longer a goal written on a yellow sticky note. It was a reality.

I worked several jobs while I was in pharmacy school. I was a nanny on weeknights. I worked as an intern at a health center pharmacy in Dorchester, and on Sundays, I was a cashier at TJ Maxx. I'm still unsure how I was able to do it all. In my fourth and final year, I completed thirty-six weeks of rotations, each six weeks long. From Brigham and Women's Hospital and Beth Israel Deaconess to Virginia Hospital Center and back to Boston. It was a long year, and I was exhausted from long days. On one rotation, I worked until ten o'clock at night, counting their pharmacy inventory.

During this time, I was also preparing to apply to residency programs across the country, and that December, I submitted a poster for the annual pharmacy midyear conference in Anaheim, California. It covered the performance improvement project on glycemic control I had completed at Virginia Hospital Center. My poster was accepted, an honor and an acknowledgment of my work, and I flew to Anaheim for a week.

The conference was also an opportunity for students to visit the booths of residency programs across the country to find out as much as we could about their respective programs. My goal that week was to visit the ten programs I was contemplating applying to and hopefully get a chance to ask their current residents what their own experiences had been like so far. There were thousands of students attending, all with the same mission. Armed with my resumes and a notepad full of questions, I hurried through the open double doors to find my first program. In a sea of black suits and professional attire, it was time to sink or swim.

Once I was done in Anaheim, I flew back to Boston and worked feverishly to complete my residency applications. The deadline was fast approaching, and I was applying to ten programs. They each required applicants write a letter of intent, provide a completed application and curriculum vitae, and answer a multitude of questions. There were also the fees to consider. The more programs I applied to, the higher the overall cost.

The night before the deadline, there was still so much left to do, and I was working past the point of exhaustion. I lay on the bathroom floor in tears, and I called my friend Justin, hoping for some sympathy.

Instead, Justin said, "Kama, get off the floor and submit your applications. Call me when you are done!"

Did he not understand I was physically and emotionally exhausted? I had been at this for four years, and I'd had enough. However, I took his advice, got very little sleep, and submitted all ten of my applications in time. The sacrifice turned out to be worth it. I received five invitations for interviews, from the Syracuse Veterans Affairs (VA) Hospital to the VA Hospital in Bangor, Maine, and three others in and around Boston. All my interviews were positive experiences, except for one.

I arrived early and was well prepared for my interview with a large academic program in Boston, which would allow me to work closely with patients in underserved communities, and I believed it would be a great fit for me. The two interviewers were both male, and we had a great conversation throughout the day. As I walked out the door at the end of the day, I happened to look back over my shoulder, and I caught the two men making inappropriate gestures at each other regarding me.

They tried to wave goodbye and pretend nothing had happened, but I felt sick to my stomach and quickly tried to find the elevator so I could get out of the building. In that moment, I decided I could not spend an entire residency year working closely with them. I wondered why women needed to be subjected to these uncomfortable situations in professional settings. This was one residency program I could not consider. I crossed them off my rank list as soon as I made it back to my apartment.

The interview process was long and expensive. For those interviews outside of Boston, I had to purchase a plane ticket and pay for hotel rooms and ground travel to and from the interviews, and I also had to pay for my meals each day. Each interview lasted almost an entire day. I over-prepared for each one and gave it everything I possibly could. For some, I had to give a presentation, so I ensured I was prepared for that too. My interview in Bangor, Maine, happened during a snowstorm, and there was no Uber from the airport to the hotel, so I took a yellow cab. It was so cold that I couldn't wait for the interview to end. After my interview at the Syracuse VA, I prayed I would match there. Most of the pharmacists who interviewed me seemed excited to meet me and were very kind. I was also familiar with Syracuse and knew I'd have a great support system in Maria and her family.

It was very important to make a great impression at every interview because five thousand students had applied for the Residency Matching Program and more than fifteen hundred would not match because of the limited number of pharmacy residencies. I believed additional residency training would provide me the clinical and leadership skills to become a more effective and confident practitioner. Additionally, I hoped it would improve my odds of obtaining a position that did not involve retail pharmacy. I had enjoyed retail pharmacy during my intern years, but there was so much more I could give to patients and I would need a different avenue by which to do it.

While interviewing for a residency position, I received a job offer for a pharmacist position at Walmart pharmacy. It was more money than I'd made in my entire life. I questioned whether I should continue with the residency process or take this job and finally have some rest. I told Justin about the job offer, and his exact words, as I remember them, were: "So you're going to pass up the most money you have ever made in your life to be a resident for little pay?"

Yes, that was exactly what I was going to do.

My intuition had never led me wrong before, and I knew it wouldn't now. I sent an email to the Walmart pharmacy district manager and I graciously turned down their generous offer. I sent up a silent prayer to the heavens and hoped I had made the right choice.

Finally, March 20th arrived, Match Day. All over the country, thousands of would-be pharmacy residents opened their email to find out which residency program they'd matched with or if they'd matched at all. I woke up early and checked my email, and there it was. I had matched at the Syracuse VA Hospital! My first choice. I was overcome with emotion. The interview process had been difficult. I'd spent hours practicing possible interview questions with Justin over the phone. He had given me feedback and made me respond to the same questions over and over. He was relentless. No wonder we were friends.

Once again, I would be moving to Syracuse—a full-circle moment. I breathed a sigh of relief, but I was anxious for the journey ahead. I knew my residency year would be challenging and imagined there would be new hills to climb.

One of my highlights of living in Boston happened on a chilly day in the spring. I was finally becoming a US citizen. My friends from pharmacy school came to my naturalization ceremony at Faneuil Hall, which we were told was known as the "Cradle of Liberty." The fact that the site had played an integral role in Boston's underground railroad network and was now the place I would take the oath of allegiance was not lost on me. It had been a long and expensive road to citizenship. I'd spent weeks studying the book of one hundred citizenship questions and answers and completed several mandatory steps before I finally received an invitation for my ceremony. It seemed like an eternity, but the day had finally arrived. I was grateful that, although I had no family in Boston who could attend, I had made friends—Nadine, Christine, and Donna—who understood the significance of the moment enough to leave class to attend with me. I will always cherish that memory.

Four years after arriving in Boston, on May 9, 2015, I walked across the stage at Gillette Stadium to accept my Doctor of Pharmacy degree. I graduated Magna Cum Laude. It was also my birthday, and I could not think of a better gift to give to myself than that moment.

I had made the dean's list every single semester, I'd won the National Association of Chain Drug Stores Award, and most importantly, I was leaving with lifelong friends and a sense of accomplishment. Our hooding ceremony and graduation ceremony occurred simultaneously. Each candidate handed their hood to a faculty member, and the advisor placed the hoods over the candidate's head to signify that we had completed our doctoral programs and were transitioning from students to colleagues.

As I walked down the steps during the hooding ceremony, I heard my family and friends screaming my name in the stands. They had come from all over the country to celebrate with me—from Milwaukee, Las Vegas, and New York City. Even my dad traveled from Florida to witness the moment, and he cried. It was an especially emotional day because my mom was able to fly to America from St. Thomas to watch me receive my degree. It was the first time she'd seen my older sister in eighteen years.

My heart was full. This was not just my achievement. The day also belonged to everyone I had met on my journey, everyone who prayed for me, who encouraged me, and who reminded me I was capable of great things. This day honored every sacrifice they had made on my behalf. It also honored my country, St. Lucia, and my grandfather, whose memory kept me going through every challenge and over every hurdle. It was for my mother, my older sister, Nadia, and Aunty Rell and her circle of prayer warriors, who prayed for hours before every single exam I had in pharmacy school. It was for every person I had met in Syracuse, Virginia, and Boston, who showed up when I needed them most. The people who opened their homes, set a place at their dining room tables, or told me they believed in me. It was for Kristin, who made sure I never went hungry during pharmacy school and who believed so much that I would succeed that she did not hesitate to co-sign for my first student loan. For Mr. Harry, who showed up on moving day and never left. For my friends who I called when the journey got too tough and I could not take one more step. For the ones who would listen without judgment and the ones who never allowed me to feel sorry for myself. It was for my village, Anse-la-Raye, the place I will always call home.

It was a momentous day, but it was not the end of the journey. Next, I needed to prepare for my licensing exam, the NAPLEX. I spent the summer after my graduation packing up my apartment in Boston, searching for a new apartment in Syracuse, and studying for the licensing and Massachusetts pharmacy law exams. It was not an easy transition to make. There was just so much to do.

CHAPTER 7

FULL-CIRCLE MOMENTS

AFTER PHARMACY SCHOOL I completed my PGY-1 residency at the Syracuse, VA Hospital. It was a year filled with opportunities to learn, to stretch, and to find my voice as a pharmacist and as a woman. Although it was a stressful year, I was grateful I found preceptors who were invested in my growth and wellbeing. I was thankful that, in addition to my co-resident Katie, I had also met some preceptors who made it a meaningful year for me. Janine, Bimpe, and Chris were especially kind to me and made sure my work-life balance did not suffer. I also met some medical residents of color during my Psych and Internal Medicine rotations who became my community. My saving grace was that I was back in Syracuse, and this time, I had a strong support system in Maria and her family. The time spent with them was the highlight of my year.

My year at the VA presented new challenges. One of my preceptors was very difficult to deal with, and over time, every interaction with him became more caustic. Finally, one morning during my four-week rotation with him, I mustered up the courage to walk into his office and tell him how he had been making me feel. "You're making this a toxic work environment," I said, "and I would really like to continue in this program, but in order for me to do this something needs to change." I was frustrated, but I remained calm. We went back and forth for a bit, but then, we finally came to an agreement. He asked that I bring it to his attention if his behavior did not change. I never had another problem with him after this conversation.

One morning, I doubled over in pain at my desk in the residents' office. It was the worst stomach pain I'd ever experienced in my life. I asked to leave work and walked to the nearby emergency room of another hospital. After several hours of tests and waiting, I was sent home with few answers. The pain worsened as the weeks went by. I lost weight. I could hardly eat. I was miserable.

My doctor suggested an endoscopy, and I was finally diagnosed with a stomach ulcer. The gastroenterologist asked me at my follow-up appointment whether there was any stress in my life. I said, "I don't think so, but I am completing my residency now." He laughed out loud and said, "You are the youngest patient I've had in a long time with a stomach ulcer. Get your stress level under control." I was dealing with a lot of stress, but I would complete this residency, stomach ulcer or not.

A few months before graduating from residency, I interviewed for a job at Froedtert Hospital in Milwaukee. I flew in for my interview and loved everyone I met on interview day. I felt I would enjoy working with this group and it would be a great opportunity to put everything I'd learned into practice. A week after completing my residency, I moved my life to Milwaukee to start work. It was truly another full-circle moment in my life. This time, however, I would not have to clean houses.

Three years after graduation, I returned to my village in St. Lucia, Anse-la-Raye, and provided ten students with scholarships to help fund their education. In my address to them, I reminded them that if I could leave a small island and move to a foreign land to chase a dream that seemed impossible for so many reasons, they were capable of anything. I informed them that I had done everything in my life scared, but I did it anyway. Seeing the hope on their faces made me want to continue doing this work of empowering students, immigrants, and young women to chase their dreams.

The students gave so much back to me that day. There was an entire ceremony planned, and some of my teachers and principals from my infant and primary school years had been invited. I hadn't seen them in more than a decade, but they all spoke about how proud they were of me and commented that my successes were not a surprise to them. My sister Nekia, her kids, and some of my cousins who live in St. Lucia were also able to attend. The students recited original poetry; they sang songs they had practiced for weeks. They thanked me for coming back to encourage them and for sowing seeds into their own educational endeavors.

Even Kristin flew from her home in NYC to be there. It was her first time traveling to St. Lucia, but because she understood the importance of this moment in my life, she did not want to miss it. It was perhaps one of the most profound and surreal moments of my life to date. I felt an immense sense of pride. Here I was, back home in my village, having done the very things I said I would do when I left.

One of the first gifts I gave myself after I became a pharmacist was a solo trip to Europe for eighteen days. Well, it didn't seem like a gift in the moment. It was actually my way of healing a broken heart—the kind of broken heart we believe will never heal and which makes us wonder whether we will ever have the capacity for love again.

I packed my bags and flew from Chicago to London. My childhood friend Abner lived there with her three daughters, so I got to spend the first few days of my trip with them. She cried when I stepped out of the Uber with my bag in hand. We hadn't seen each other in nineteen years.

It was a busy time in London, as the royal wedding would be taking place the following week. There was so much to see in so little time. I saw *The Lion King* in London's theater district, the West End; took a boat tour of the River Thames; and spent hours at Windsor Castle, Stonehenge, Bath, and the Tate Modern museum. I got lost in Shoreditch, trying to find a restaurant with several five-star reviews, and the food was worth getting lost for. I even flew to Scotland, where I spent five hours sightseeing before I flew back to London.

Rome was the next stop on my journey, and walking into the Colosseum took my breath away. It was a rainy day in Rome, but I hardly noticed. Every piazza amazed me; each one held more magic to behold. I made a wish at Trevi Fountain and made stops at the Roman Forum, the Pantheon, and St. Peter's Basilica and rested on the Spanish Steps. I woke up extra early on a Sunday and braved the crowds at Vatican Square to watch the Pope say Mass. Some of my best memories of food are now centered around Rome. I had never had pizza or pasta or wine like I enjoyed in Rome. It was a holy experience.

I woke up on my birthday in a Paris hotel. I was alone and incredibly happy. My feet were sore from exploring the Champs-Élysées, the Eiffel Tower, and the Palace of Versailles. I did any and everything I could possibly fit into two days. I lit candles and said my prayers at Notre Dame Cathedral. When I was too exhausted to walk, I took a boat tour of the Seine River and watched the city unfold from a new perspective.

My excitement was palpable when the small plane landed in Toulouse, France, and I saw my friend Fatima and her husband walking towards me at the airport. So much had happened since I last saw her, and she was now pregnant with twins. We had the best time catching up and reminiscing about our time in Boston. We laughed for hours. I had missed her.

My final stop was Barcelona. This time, I would have to see the city by rickshaw since I only had twenty-four hours left before I returned home. My driver made sure I experienced Gaudi's breathtaking architecture, especially the immaculate Basílica de la Sagrada Família. I explored the fountains of La Rambla and the Gothic Quarter and ate exquisite paella on the beach. In my final hours, I took in all of Mercat de la Boquería, and it was the best kind of sensory overload. The delicious aromas of tapas enveloped the market. Every inch of space was covered in the most vibrant colors of fruits and vegetables.

Everything hit me all at once, and before I knew it, I was sobbing in the middle of an outdoor market in Barcelona. I wasn't crying because I was exhausted or unhappy. I cried because my heart was full and I felt what I could only describe as a state of peace. My tears were an act of worship. How had this become my life?

Every woman should travel alone at least once in her life. I learned so much during my eighteen days in Europe. I was a woman who truly enjoyed my own company, a woman who could make her dreams come true and reward herself for her countless years of sacrifice. I gave myself grace when I needed to and reminded myself that I had created this beautiful life. I was no longer in survival mode. My promise on my plane ride back to Chicago was that I would never return to survival mode. I would choose myself above all else and live a full life.

There are days when I ask myself, "How did I go from an immigrant who cleaned houses to a doctorate in pharmacy?" The same answers keep coming back to me. I remained focused. I found a dream that would not die. A dream that kept me up at night. A dream I needed to accomplish. A dream that allowed me to be in service to others.

I owned my story—all of it—including the moments that were difficult, traumatic, and painful. I also embraced the moments when God showed up for me and restored my faith. In all things, through every hurdle, I counted my blessings.

There was never a moment along my journey when I wasn't aware of the incredible blessings I received along the way, including every person who appeared when I needed them the most to lend a helping hand or who offered me a place of shelter and rest. I realized everything happening in my life was happening for me. For my greatest good.

Even the darkest moments of my life helped shape my future. Nothing was wasted. I understood my journey would get tough, but I was determined to never give up and to lean on my faith when I needed it most. Through it all, I learned the meaning of resiliency and what it means to stand firmly in the face of every adversity.

Yes, I sacrificed. Some years, I needed to sacrifice relationships, friendships, time, and energy on the road to making my dream a reality. Those were difficult decisions to make but were well worth it when I crossed the finish line. Not everyone who began my journey with me has remained in my life, and I have learned that this too is okay. I don't make homes out of people like I used to. I have learned to simply experience them as they come and go. The ones who remain are the ones who were meant to be here in my life.

What I know for sure is that it is our birthright to live a life of abundance and peace—a life in which our greatest dreams are realized. There are countless lessons I have learned along the way, and I hope you will find them useful as you go through your own journey.

FIVE LESSONS TO TAKE WITH YOU AS YOU GO

Stay open to pivoting on your journey towards your dream. I always envisioned myself as a doctor but didn't realize I would be a Doctor of Pharmacy. I embraced the pivot and have found a life of purpose and balance. I am committed to the patients I serve, the students I take on rotation, and the communities I educate through my speaking. I know now I am not just a pharmacist. I am also an educator, and that has brought me an even greater sense of fulfillment.

Express gratitude. What has served me well in my life is to live in a constant state of gratitude. No one I have met on my journey needed to show any kindness to me, but so many people did, and for that I remain grateful. I make it a point to say thank you for any kindness I receive and to find a way to pay it forward.

Be in service to others. A purposeful life is one in which you are in service to others. I'm grateful I have chosen a career in healthcare because it allows me to use my skills to improve the lives of my patients and to be an advocate for them when they are unable to articulate their own needs.

Forgive easily. Perhaps this has been the hardest lesson I've learned but also the most beneficial. I know now that everyone we meet is fighting their own inner battles. Of course, I've experienced heartbreak, disappointment, crushing betrayals, and trauma, but I refused to remain in that place of hurt. I have learned to release it all in love, which has enabled me to finally experience a peace that surpasses all understanding. I believe everyone is doing the very best they can, and we are all works in progress. I have forgiven people who are probably not aware of the level of hurt they caused me. At twenty-six, I went to therapy for the first time. At our final session together, my therapist, a woman named Rebecca, told me, "Kama, I'm not sure who you will become in the world, but I know I will see your name in lights." My goal for therapy was to experience one day of peace, and I can say for sure that I've had weeks, months, and years of peace.

We are not meant to wear our traumas as a safety blanket. We're meant to live in a place of wholeness and healing. I've learned that, even if I never achieve another dream for the rest of my life, I am enough. As I am.

Keep the faith. Faith is the promise that my best days are still ahead of me, that every step of my journey has prepared me for what lies ahead. It is a quiet confidence that I am seen and known and that God's greatest desire for me is to live fully in a place of abundance. For that and all my blessings, I am grateful.

IN GRATITUDE

NO ONE PREPARES YOU for the rollercoaster ride of becoming an author. I have done hard things. But this is probably one of the hardest. None of this would be possible without the people I am going to name below.

For my parents, who I now firmly believe gave me all of what they believed was their very best at the time. Although I did not come to this realization until I was thirty years old, I am glad I did. This simple truth set me free. For my mother, who made the ultimate sacrifice out of love, all of my strength, resilience, and generous spirit come from you. Thank you.

I am grateful for every moment I have gotten to share with all my siblings and their amazing children and spouses. Especially Nadia and Orville. I am humbled that we get to experience this life together. I'm grateful for all my incredibly gifted and talented nieces and nephews all over the world. Thank you all so much!

For Aunty Rell and Aunty Margo, who have always cheered me on and cared deeply for me. And for all my aunts, uncles, and cousins all over the world, especially all my cousins and cousins-in-law in Milwaukee, who have so graciously agreed to host my book signing (Amanda, Gether, Sherlan, Reynelle, DJ Catola, Nando, yes Shane even you, lol). I am grateful to all of you.

For everyone along my journey in America who showed up when it seemed all hope would be lost. Lien Lee, the Morgan family, the Mejia family, Pat Bliss, Maria and Maryellen, Hetty and Susan, Marin and Marley, Janine Kozak, Mr. Harry, Dr. Makuja, Kay Tucker, Dr. Mireku. Thank you will never suffice.

For my friends, old and new, who have stood with me and by me through the tests of time. Kristin (everyone deserves a friend like you), Justin (by an act of God we've made it to chapter 13 and I am so grateful), Lervan, Shanasse, Abner, Natalie, Amirh, Donna, Maritza, Rama, Fatima, Angie, Andy, Teresa, Bethany, Michelle, and Dez. For the names I have not listed, please know you are equally important to me and you are kept in my best thoughts. Many, many thanks!

For my entire Froedtert family, it has been a pleasure to work with you over the years. In or out of a pandemic, you are the most incredible team, and I am in awe of everything you give to patients daily.

For every teacher, professor, mentor, and preceptor who sowed seeds that birthed the woman I am becoming. Thank you.

Thank you to Patrice Washington who told me that my story was not simply a typical immigrant story and that it was a story that should be told—that my story was not for me; it was to set someone else free. May it be so.

For my editor, Candice L Davis, who asked for several more words. You were right. Thank you for asking for more.

To every reader, I hope this book has found you well. Maybe you are in need of some inspiration or encouragement. Here is your reminder that you can do hard things. The past does not equal your future. Every day is another chance to begin again. To find the dream that will not die.

For my grandfather, the kindest most generous soul I have ever known. I pray you are proud.

To God Be the Gory.
March 24th, 2021 1:54 AM
Milwaukee, WI

Made in the USA
Monee, IL
21 July 2021

74070612R00066